EAST Meets WEST

by Joseph Rahim

Harcourt

Orlando   Boston   Dallas   Chicago   San Diego

Visit *The Learning Site!*
www.harcourtschool.com

Early Traders

People have always used ships to travel the oceans. Long ago, people wanted to learn more about their world. They traveled in ships to new lands to meet new people.

Some ships were light for traveling on rivers. Others were heavy, with sails made of colorful cloth. The best ships were fast and strong. They could sail well in any kind of weather.

The captains of these ships often did not know where land was. Life at sea could be difficult. The oceans were rough and the winds were strong. The sailors had to be very brave. Sometimes they were gone from home for many months.

The compass was a very important tool for sailors. Because it always pointed the way North, ship captains could find their way home from distant lands.

Mapping the World

Those early sailors were explorers, too. They always looked for an easier, better way to reach distant lands. They needed a guide to help them find their way home. What if a storm should carry their ships far away from where they wanted to be?

The explorers began to write down how far they were going, and the best way to travel from place to place. They began to make maps of their journeys. Over time, explorers made better maps of the world.

Maps are important tools. They show us the location of the land and the oceans. They show us the distance from place to place.

The first maps showed a very different world than today's maps. More lands were discovered over time and the maps changed. Slowly, maps began to show the seven continents and the four oceans. Maps began to show important cities and the location of lakes and rivers.

The Exploration of America

The Vikings were good map makers. They sailed their ships, which were very long, across the Atlantic Ocean. The Vikings controlled the oceans for many years.

In the 1400s and 1500s, explorers set out from the continent of Europe. They wanted to sail to the Far East. They wanted to bring back different kinds of goods. One such explorer was named Christopher Columbus. He dreamed of finding an easy way to the East Indies. He sailed across the Atlantic Ocean. He did not have a map.

After months at sea, he spotted land. Columbus thought it was the East Indies, but he had really found a new world. This new world was later named America.

    The discovery of America was a great surprise to everyone. At that time, people in Europe thought that the world was flat. They thought that they would fall off the edge of the earth if they sailed too far. Columbus's trip showed that the world was really round!

    By the early 1600s many people wanted to see the new world. They dreamed of a better life. They began to leave Europe. They sailed west across the Atlantic Ocean. They hoped to make a better life in the new land. Soon thousands of new families were living in America.

7

Clipper Ships

People learned how to build faster and better sailing ships. Clipper ships were the most beautiful of all. They were first built in America in the 1800s. Clipper ships had many large sails. They could move fast in a good wind. When the winds were quiet, clipper ships had so many sails that they could keep moving.

The first clipper ships were built to sail from the port of New York City to the Far East. They brought back tea from China.

The California Gold Rush!

In 1848 gold was discovered in California. All over America people shouted, "Go west!" At that time travel across land was very difficult. There were no trains to California. There were no roads or maps to guide the way. Many people traveled to California by clipper ships.

The clipper ships left New York City, traveled around the continent of South America, then sailed up to California.

Many people thought that they would find gold right away. Only a few people were lucky.

In California many sailors ran away from their ships. They wanted to find gold, too. The ship captains had to find new sailors to finish the trip.

After the Gold Rush many people decided to stay in California. They built homes and farmed the land. They were glad to have made the journey west.

From Sail to Steam

By the late 1800s, ships with steam engines became a better way to travel across the seas than sailing ships. They were faster and could carry more people. Ships were built of steel, not wood or iron. Steel was lighter and stronger.

Soon thousands of people were leaving the continent of Europe to come to America. Most people arrived by steamship in New York City. Many of the people who made the trip dreamed of making a better life for their families in America. Their dreams came true when they saw the Statue of Liberty.

New Hope in America

People came to America from many different countries. They had different hopes and dreams. Some people wanted jobs. Some wanted a chance to own land. Others wanted freedom to live life their own way.

They were told that America's streets were made of gold. They were told that life would be easy. They were filled with hope and eager to follow their dreams.

But life was very difficult for most people. They spoke different languages. It was hard to find work. They tried to fit into American life. But many times, people who came to America were not treated well. They worked in factories or coal mines. They worked long hours for little pay.

But America was still a land of hope for them. Life was better, even though the streets were not paved with gold.

New York wasn't the only city where people entered the United States. In the 1960s many people came from Asia to the West Coast. They often lived in the western states of California and Washington.

They came by ships and by airplane. They came with hopes and dreams. Some people wanted to find better work. Others wanted the freedom to live as they chose.

Ships have always been important. They carried people across the oceans. They still do.

The captains still use maps to find their way. Today's ships are larger, with bigger rooms for sleeping than the Viking ships. They carry more people, and they are much faster. The journey from Europe to New York only takes a few days.

Today's ships carry more than people. They carry fruits, meat, vegetables, machines, cars, and sometimes even other ships.

Ships have brought people closer together. They have made dreams come true.